HERE COMES
SUPER BUS 3

Pupil's Book

María José Lobo

◆

Pepita Subirà

MACMILLAN

Contents

1 Listen and order 📼

a

b

c

d

e

f

g

Hello, children!

Little Red Hen   Julie   Greenman   crazy computer   Professor Memo   Jane   James

2 Song 📼

SCHOOL

Run, run, run
Fast, fast, fast

Summer is over
Autumn is here
Now we're beginning
A new school year

Run, run, run
Fast, fast, fast

We're back in class
With Super Bus
Hello! Hello!
From all of us

Run, run, run
Fast, fast, fast

10 SCHOOL

◆ 3

3 Play and say

Concentrate.

6 Listen, point and speak 🔈

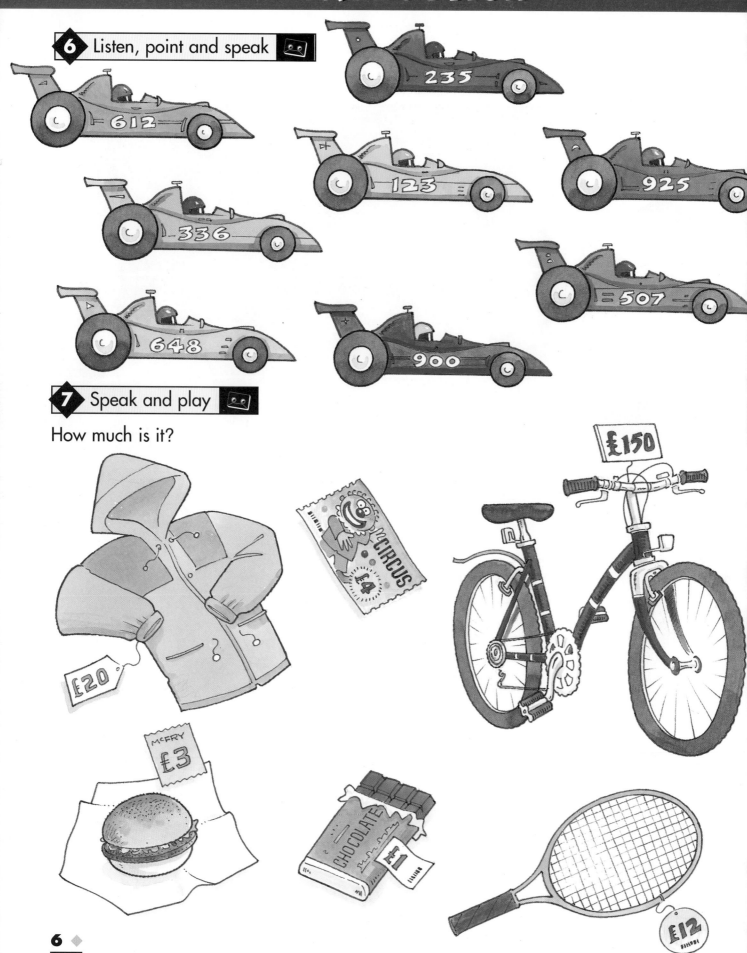

7 Speak and play 🔈

How much is it?

1

POEMS AND CONTESTS

1 Listen and say 📼   Have you got …?

Music

Geography

History

PE

English

Art

Sports

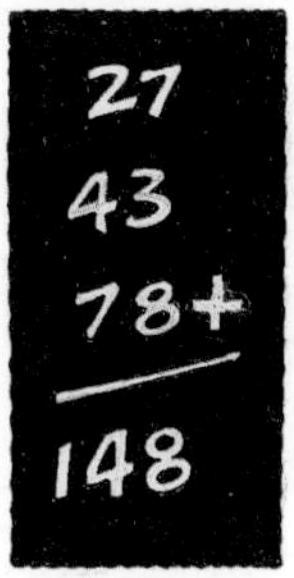

27
43
78+
───
148

Maths

French

2 Listen and repeat 📼   What time is it?

1 — five past nine

2 — ten past five

3 — twenty past three

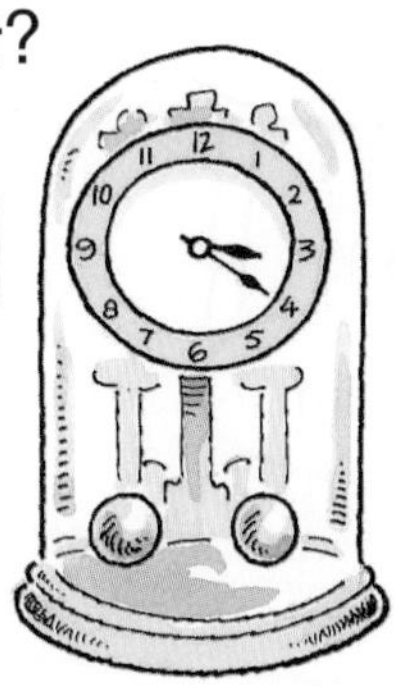

4 — twenty-five past four

5 — twenty-five to eight

6 — twenty to ten

7 — ten to twelve

8 — five to one

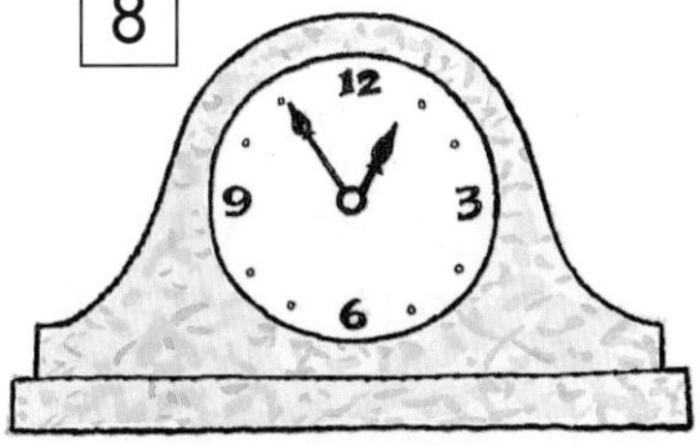

 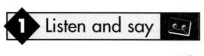
I love milk shakes!
Grandma likes cakes
Grandpa likes grapes
Dad likes steaks
And I like milk shakes

Colours
Yellow and red
Green and blue
Purple is my favourite
What about you?

At school!
Emma likes History
Music and PE
Harry likes Drama
French and Geography

2 Listen and find out

Is it Lucy or Paul's timetable?

Hi, I'm Lucy.

Hi, I'm Paul.

	Monday	Tuesday	Wednesday	Thursday	Friday
9.00	English	Swimming	English	Geography	English
9.50	History		History	Sports	History
10.40			B R E A K		
11.10	Maths	Geography	Maths	French	Maths
12.00			L U N C H		
1.30	Art	English	French	Music	P.E.
2.30		Science	Science		

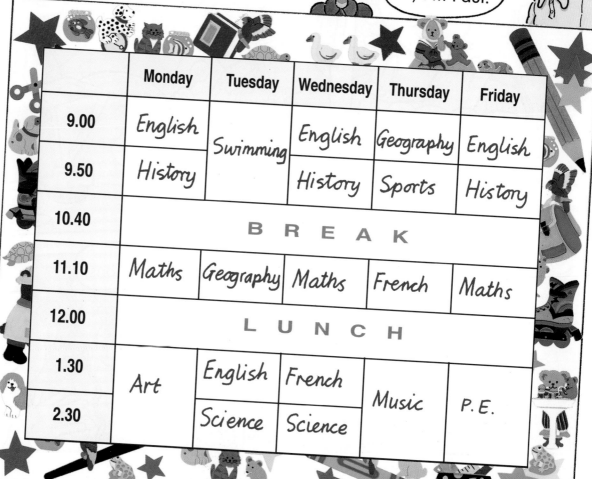

3 | Make your school timetable   You need: a pen   crayons

1

draw the times

2

write the subjects

	MON	TUES	WEDS	THURS	FRI
🕐	Maths	Art	Maths	Swimming	Maths
🕐	Geography		Geography		Geography
🕐	B R E A K				
🕐	French	English	English	English	English
🕐	L U N C H				
🕐	P.E.	History	Music	Science	History
🕐		Sports		French	Science

3 | decorate your timetable

4 | Song

Friday, Friday
Is my favourite day
The weekend's here
And I can play, play, play

History at nine
Maths at ten to ten
Swimming in the pool
Then back to school again

Music and PE
Till half past three
Then, at last, home
To play and watch TV

Friday, Friday
Is my favourite day
The weekend's here
And I can play, play, play

...day
Tuesday
Wednesday
Thursday
Friday
Saturday
Sunday

11

DO YOU KNOW THAT...?

1 Listen and read

1 Nursery rhymes are old poems for little children.

2 Many poems are 'action rhymes'. This means that you do an action when you say the poem.

My house is big and warm. Come in and close the door.

3 Some poems are in shapes.

4 There are 65 alphabets in the world.

This is some of the Roman alphabet.

MAGRIPPALFCOSTERTIVMFECIT

This is some of the Greek alphabet.

Τυχερὸ κι ἄτυχο πλάσμα
στη ζωή την ἄχαρη ...
ΤΥΧΕΡΟ ΚΙ ΑΤΥΧΟ
ΠΛΑΣΜΑ ΣΤΗ...
ΔΕΚΑΤΡΕΙΣ ΦΩΤΙΕΣ
ΨΥΧΕΣ ΚΑΙ ΣΩΜΑΤΑ

This is some of the Arabic alphabet.

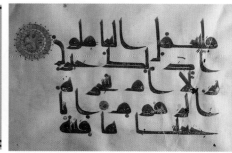

2 COMPUTER TIME

1 Listen and say

1st	first
2nd	second
3rd	third
4th	fourth
5th	fifth
6th	sixth
7th	seventh
8th	eighth
9th	ninth
10th	tenth
11th	eleventh
12th	twelfth
13th	thirteenth
14th	fourteenth
15th	fifteenth
16th	sixteenth
17th	seventeenth
18th	eighteenth
19th	nineteenth
20th	twentieth

2 Moving game

Look, listen and do.

switch on

On
Off

switch off

click

mouse

return key

printer

press

13

The Crazy COMPUTER

| Look, listen and read | It is computer time. The children are working in groups. They are playing language games on the computers. Karen and John are playing with a new computer! |

Wow! A new computer!

Switch it on, Karen.

1

The children follow the instructions very carefully.

Click on the mouse.

Welcome to the 222 Game

Ha!

How many points can you score in two minutes?

Oh! The computer's laughing!

2

Ready? Let's begin. Letters:

Ha

a, b, c ...

3

Try ordinal numbers now. Listen:

Ha!

1st, 2nd, 3rd ...

ON   OFF

4

1 Listen and play

2 Computer rap

Switch me on

Click on the mouse

Play the 222 Game

What comes next?

Well done! Very good!

Not bad! Try again!

Not very good! Wrong!

Sorry, but I've won!

3 Listen and speak

What are they doing?

1 Who's speaking?
2 What's the clown doing?
3 What are the dogs doing?
4 Who's throwing balls in the air and catching them?
5 Who's swinging?

4 Play the Chain Game

Take a flashcard and mime the action.

He's hopping, you're dancing and I'm ...

You're hopping and I'm dancing.

I'm hopping.

5 Listen and speak

What games do you like?

chess

cards

computer games

dominoes

draughts

board games

6 Make picture dominoes

Cut outs 1 and 2   Activity Book pages 67 and 69

You need: crayons   a pair of scissors

1 colour

2 cut out

They're dancing

3 play

He's laughing

She's swimming

It's running

They're playing

DO YOU KNOW THAT...?

1 Listen and read

1 This is a photo of the first computer. It is 30 metres long and 3 metres high, and it weighs 30,000 kilos.

2 Some portable computers are very small.

3 A virus is a set of instructions in a computer programme. A virus can destroy computer programmes and your work!

4 Robots can imitate human and animal actions. A computer programme controls the actions of the robots. This robot can run, play and bark like a dog.

5 Surfing the internet is good fun. You can get lots of information and buy and sell things through the internet.

3

SPACE

planets

the Moon

the Sun

the Earth

a comet

stars

2 Riddle 📼   Listen and guess.

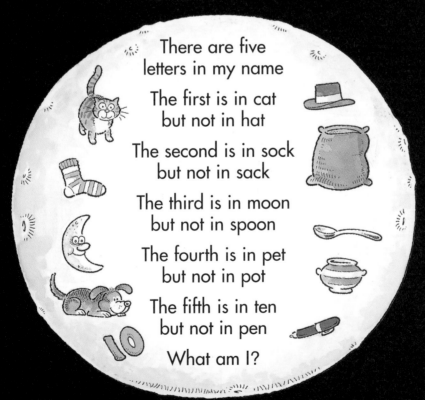

There are five
letters in my name

The first is in cat
but not in hat

The second is in sock
but not in sack

The third is in moon
but not in spoon

The fourth is in pet
but not in pot

The fifth is in ten
but not in pen

What am I?

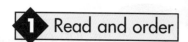

1 Read and order

a Mum reads the news about the comet.

b Julie can see the comet and lots of stars!

c It's Saturday.

d Julie walks up the hill in slippers.

e They go to Mossy Hill to see the comet.

2 Make a collage

You need: thin cardboard magazine pages

scissors crayons glue

1 draw

2 cut

3 stick

4 describe your picture

a He can't swim.
d She can play football.

b She can't skate.
e She can dive.

c They can climb.
f He can't ride a bike.

4 Song 🔊

Tell me, tell me
What can you do?

What can I do?
I'll tell you

I can jump up and down
I can turn round and round
I can hop, I can skip
I can swim, I can wink

Tell me, tell me
What can't you do?

What can't I do?
I'll tell you

I can't fly in the sky
I can't jump very high
I can't skate, I can't dive
I can't climb, I can't drive

◆ **23**

Look at the …, miss a turn.   ? Ask: Can you …?

DO YOU KNOW THAT...?

1 Listen and read

1 A galaxy is a group of millions of stars.
The name of our galaxy is the Milky Way.
Every year new stars appear in the Milky Way.

2 All stars are round but they are not the same colour and size. There are blue, white, yellow, orange and red stars. Old stars are red. The Sun is a yellow star.

3 This is the first man to walk on the moon in the year 1969. His name is Neil Armstrong. The footprints of the astronauts will be visible on the moon for thousands of years.

4 Halley's comet is very big. The tail of the comet is thousands of kilometres long. Halley's comet appears every 76 years.

5 Mars is a very important planet. This is the NASA Pathfinder on Mars in July 1997.

... left...

Where's the dog?

... right...

in the cupboard

on the sofa

next to the TV

behind the armchair

between the bookcase and the sofa

in front of the TV

under the table

... out of...
... over ...

2 Moving game

Listen and do.

Professor MEMO

Look, listen and read

In the offices of the *Bad and Worse Company*, two men are talking …

Good and Better are making a new helicopter. Jim, go and steal the plans.

But that's impossible!

1

You're a computer expert.

2

Jim takes a gun and leaves in his car.

3

It is very late. Professor Memo is finishing the helicopter plans for the *Good and Better Company*. His dog, Brainy, is with him. Brainy is very intelligent.

4

Well, the helicopter plans are finished. It's very late. Let's go home.

WOOF!

WOOF!

Where's my bag?

Now, where are my glasses?

The computer's on.

The light's on.

5

1 Tell the story

1 2 3 4 5 6

2 Act out the story

3 Rap

Where are my shoes?
They're behind the door
Where are my socks?
They're on the floor

Where's my hat?
It's under the bed
Where are my glasses?
They're on my head

What's the time?
It's five past eight
Where's my bag?
Oh, no! I'm late!

5 Listen and speak Clare's day.

a car

1 get up

2 have breakfast

b helicopter

c boat

3 go to school

4 have lunch

d train

5 go home

6 help

e bus

7 read or watch TV

8 go to bed

6 Ask and answer Talk about Clare's day.

f bicycle

What time does Clare get up?

She gets up at eight o'clock.

Does Clare read a book?

Yes, she does.

g plane

7 Play the Blah Blah Game

DO YOU KNOW THAT...?

1 The Spanish AVE is a very fast train. It goes from Madrid to Seville in two and a half hours.

2 Concorde is a very fast plane. It flies from London to New York in three hours.

3 The Orient Express is a famous and expensive train. It goes from London to Venice. A return ticket London–Venice–London costs about £2,000.

4 You can go from France to England by train. Le Shuttle is the train that goes under the sea.

5 Helicopters are not very fast but they can fly forwards, backwards and sideways.

5

THE WEATHER

1

TRACKS CYCLING CLUB

CYCLE WITH US TO
MOSSY HILL!
THE GREATEST
ADVENTURE ...
ON YOUR BICYCLE!

SATURDAY 10th at 8 A.M.
Children from 11 to 14.
Telephone Angela (345 321)

2

WALTON YOUTH CLUB

VISIT TO ROCKY ZOO GR-R-R-R-R-R-EAT ADVENTURES!

Bus leaves the Youth Club at
7 on Sunday morning.
To reserve your place phone
605 604 (Miss Tamer)

3

HEIGHTS WALKING CLUB

Do you like walking? Then come to
Mossy Caves — ON FOOT!

Visit the caves ... have a great picnic
... play lots of games!

Saturday 10th, start at 7.30 A.M.
Contact Mr Randall (718 728)

Where are they going?
How are they going?
When are they going?
What time are they going?

LONELY HOUSE

1 Mr Stanton is taking the Lions Sports Club on an adventure weekend. There is a new girl, Jane. She is very shy.

Jane, this is Joe. This is Anna, Julia and Steven, and this is Victor.

Hello!

Hello!

Hello!

LIONS SPORTS CLUB
ADVENTURE WEEKEND
Open to all members aged 10–14 years.
Bus leaves Saturday 9 AM, returns Sunday 6 PM.
If you are interested, see Mr Stanton.

2 Right everybody! Look at your maps.

3 Jane's nice.

Yes, but she looks very shy.

4 Here we are!

5 It is dark now. The children are in Lonely House.

Come on, Jane. Tell us a story. It's your turn.

Oh, no … I can't.

OK. I'll tell you a story. Listen …

1 Chant 📼

In a dark, dark forest
there's a dark, dark house

And in the dark, dark house
there's a dark, dark room

And in the dark, dark room
there's a dark, dark cupboard

And in the dark, dark cupboard
there's … a GHOST!!

2 Listen, do and speak 📼   What do they say in the story?

3 Listen and say 📼   What are you afraid of?

Are you afraid of *snakes*?

Yes, I am.

No, I'm not.

1 snakes

2 spiders

3 dogs

4 storms

5 horror films

6 ghosts

7 monsters

8 rats

4 Listen and do 🔊   What's the weather like?

1 It's sunny

2 It's raining

3 It's windy

4 It's foggy

5 It's snowing

6 It's cloudy

5 Play and say   Memory game.

Cut out 4   Activity Book page 73

You need: ✂️ scissors   ✏️ crayons

It's raining.

6 Song 🔊

If it's sunny and you know it
  run outside
If it's sunny and you know it
  run outside
If it's sunny and you know it
And you really want to enjoy it
If it's sunny and you know it
  run outside

If it's raining and you know it
  splash about …

If it's windy and you know it fly
  your kite …

DO YOU KNOW THAT...?

1 A storm is a period of very bad weather. Rain, strong winds, snow, hail, thunder and lightning are normally part of a storm. Do not stand under a tree in a thunderstorm.

2 Thunder and lightning occur at the same time, but we see the lightning first and then we hear the thunder because light travels faster than sound.
One second between seeing lightning and hearing thunder means a distance of about 340 metres between you and the storm.

3 Hurricanes are strong winds. Hurricanes are also called typhoons or cyclones. A hurricane can travel at 300 km per hour. It can destroy houses and kill people.

4 Tornadoes are also very strong winds. They are smaller than hurricanes but they are more destructive.

6
MY NEIGHBOURHOOD

1 Memory game   What's in the picture?

traffic lights

bus stop

postbox

zebra crossing

telephone box

litter bin

bottle bank

Is there a	bottle bank?	Yes, there is a *bottle bank*.
	hotel?	No, there isn't a *hotel*.

Are there any	traffic lights?	Yes, there are some *traffic lights*.
	motorbikes?	No, there aren't any *motorbikes*.

◆ 39

DUSTBIN PLANET

Look, listen and read

This is Dustbin Planet. The pollution here is very bad. There is a lot of rubbish on the ground and the smell is horrible. People live in skyscrapers and they wear oxygen masks.

The Sun doesn't shine on Dustbin Planet. It is dark. There aren't any trees.

There aren't any flowers. Everything is dead.

The rivers are dirty. The seas are dirty. There is rubbish everywhere: plastic bags, paper, bottles, tins, cans …

It is Monday morning. Three children are walking to school.

Look! What's this?

I think it's a flower.

It isn't dead! It's alive!

It needs some light and water. What can we do?

1 Listen, repeat and act out 📼

2 Listen and choose 📼   What does Greenman say, a or b?

1 a Don't clean your planet.
   b Clean your planet.

2 a Don't throw rubbish in the rivers.
   b Throw rubbish in the rivers.

3 a Don't put rubbish in bins.
   b Put rubbish in bins.

4 a Don't put bottles in bottle banks.
   b Put bottles in bottle banks.

3 Song 📼

Don't throw paper away
Keep that tin

Don't throw bottles away
Put rubbish in the bin

Please keep the Earth clean!
Please keep the Earth green!

Recycle your old paper
Recycle every tin

Put bottles in the bottle bank
Put rubbish in the bin

Please keep the Earth clean!
Please keep the Earth green!

4 Make posters

You need: thin cardboard   magazines
scissors   crayons   glue

1
Green is BEAUTIFUL!

2
RECYCLE PAPER BAGS
Save Trees

3
I love Sunshine

4
I DON'T WANT your LITTER

5
Big and small we love them all

1 Listen and read

1 The Mediterranean Sea is very polluted. In some places it is very dirty and you can't swim.

2 Every week we need the wood of thousands of trees to make paper for newspapers.

3 The fumes from cars and buses are a serious problem in lots of big cities.

4 A family of four members produces about 1,750 kg of rubbish a year. About 600 kg of this rubbish is paper, glass bottles, cans, tins and plastic bags that can be recycled.

5 Green groups organize campaigns against pollution. They want to protect the Earth. Greenpeace and Friends of the Earth are green organizations.

Little Red Hen

Look, listen and read 📼

Narrator: Little Red Hen lives on a farm with her chicks. One day she finds some wheat.
Little Red Hen: Look, children! This is wheat!

Narrator: Little Red Hen decides to plant the wheat. But it is very hard work, and she asks for help.
Little Red Hen: Hello, Mr Dog. Can you help me to plant this wheat?
Mr Dog: Woof! Woof! Sorry, but I'm ill. I've got toothache.
Little Red Hen: Oh! Get better soon.
Mr Dog: Thank you. I'm not ill. But I don't want to work.

Narrator: Little Red Hen asks Mr Pig.
Little Red Hen: Hello, Mr Pig. Can you help me to plant this wheat?
Mr Pig: Oink! Oink! Sorry, but I'm ill. I've got tummyache.
Little Red Hen: Oh! Get better soon.
Mr Pig: Thank you. I'm not ill. But I don't want to work.

Narrator: Little Red Hen asks Mr Duck.

Little Red Hen: Hello, Mr Duck. Can you help me to plant this wheat?

Mr Duck: Quack! Quack! Sorry, but I'm ill. I've got a headache.

Little Red Hen: Oh! Get better soon.

Mr Duck: Thank you. I'm not ill. But I don't want to work.

Narrator: Mr Dog, Mr Pig and Mr Duck don't help Little Red Hen. So she plants the wheat all by herself. Dig, dig, dig …

Little Red Hen: Finished! But I'm very tired!

Narrator: Now the wheat is tall and strong. It is time to cut it. Little Red Hen asks for help again.

Little Red Hen: Who can help me to cut the wheat?

Mr Dog: Woof! Woof! Sorry, I've got toothache.

Mr Pig: Oink! Oink! Sorry, I've got tummyache.

Mr Duck: Quack! Quack! Sorry, I've got a headache.

Narrator: Mr Dog, Mr Pig and Mr Duck don't help Little Red Hen. So she cuts the wheat all by herself. Cut, cut, cut …

Little Red Hen: Finished! But I'm very tired!

Narrator: Now it is time to make the flour. Little Red Hen asks for help again.

Little Red Hen: Who can help me to make the flour?

Mr Dog: Woof! Woof! Sorry, I've got toothache.

Mr Pig: Oink! Oink! Sorry, I've got tummyache.

Mr Duck: Quack! Quack! Sorry, I've got a headache.

Narrator: Mr Dog, Mr Pig and Mr Duck don't help Little Red Hen. So she makes the flour all by herself. Grind, grind, grind …

Little Red Hen: Finished! But I'm very tired!

Narrator: Now it is time to make the bread. Little Red Hen asks for help again.

Little Red Hen: Who can help me to make the bread?

Mr Dog: Woof! Woof! Sorry, I've got toothache.

Mr Pig: Oink! Oink! Sorry, I've got tummyache.

Mr Duck: Quack! Quack! Sorry, I've got a headache.

Narrator: Mr Dog, Mr Pig and Mr Duck don't help Little Red Hen. So she makes the bread all by herself. Bake, bake, bake …

Little Red Hen: Finished! It smells delicious!

Mr Dog, Mr Pig, Mr Duck: Can we have some bread?

Little Red Hen: No, you can't. You're ill! This bread is for me and my chicks.

Narrator: And Little Red Hen and her chicks eat the bread. And Mr Dog, Mr Pig and Mr Duck have nothing.

2 Song

Doctor, doctor
What can I do?
I've got earache
And a cold, too
I've got tummyache
Have I got flu?

Doctor, doctor
What can I do?
I've got a headache
And a cough, too
I've got a sore throat
Have I got flu?

Yes, you've got flu
This is what you can do
Go and lie down
Stay quiet, don't move
Don't play, just rest
No school for you!

DOCTOR BROWN

3 Listen and do the roleplay

It's Monday. Let's call the register. Sarah?

She's not in class. She's ill.

She's got toothache.

What's the matter with Sarah?

REGISTER

Healthy habits

Healthy habits prevent illnesses. Eat the right food, do lots of exercise and keep your body clean.

These foods are good for you:

meat and fish   fruit and vegetables   milk and cheese   rice, pasta and cereals.

Sugar is bad for your teeth. Don't eat lots of chocolates and sweets.

Walking and playing sports are good forms of exercise.

Watching TV for hours and hours, and going to bed late are bad habits.

Washing your hair and body regularly,

brushing your teeth

and washing your hands before eating are good habits.

DO YOU KNOW THAT...?

1 Listen and read

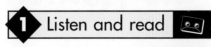

1 Bread, sugar, tea, coffee and chocolate come from plants.

2 We make bread, cakes, biscuits and pasta from wheat. Wheat is a grass plant. It is about one metre tall.

3 Sugar comes from two plants. One is sugar cane, a giant grass plant, and the other is sugar beet.

4 Chocolate and coffee come from beans. Cocoa beans are the fruit of the cacao tree. We make chocolate from cocoa beans. Coffee beans are the fruit of the coffee tree.

5 We make tea from the leaves of a small bush.

2 Board game

The Health Game

You need: dice counters

START

Do you …? Yes, I do … No, I don't …

You're ill. Miss a turn.

THANKSGIVING

1 Listen and read

The Pilgrim Story

1. These are the Pilgrims. They come from England. This is their ship, the Mayflower. It is the year 1620.

2. They are in America now.
   My son, this is America!
   Hooray!

3. But after some months …
   I'm very hungry.
   Our plants don't grow.
   I'm hungry too.

4. The Indians help the Pilgrims.
   This is corn.
   Corn is good here.

5. Now the corn is very tall.

6. Thank you for your help, friends.

2 Listen and speak

Thank you.

Thank you.
Thank you very much.
Thanks.
Thanks a lot.

Here you are.

THE MAYFLOWER

3 Write   Cut out 5   Activity Book page 75

You need: scissors   crayons

1 cut out

2 write and colour

Thursday 26th

3 make a class book

Thursday 26th
Isabel
Thank you very much
for the book.
I like it very much.
David

1 Listen and read

1 Thanksgiving Day is a very important festival in Canada and in the U.S.A.

CANADA

U.S.A.

2 In Canada, they celebrate Thanksgiving Day on the second Monday of October.

3 In the U.S.A., they celebrate Thanksgiving Day on the fourth Thursday of November.

4 On Thanksgiving Day, many people eat turkey and pumpkin pie.

2 Make a cracker

You need: a cardboard tube   thin paper

coloured paper   ribbon   scissors   presents

1 write a poem

*Christmas is here,
And the New Year*

2 cut the tube in the middle

3 put the present and the poem inside the tube

4 roll the thin paper around the tube

5 tie the ends with ribbon

6 cut the ends and decorate the cracker with the coloured paper

3 Song

Rudolf the red-nosed reindeer
Had a very shiny nose
And if you ever saw it
You would even say it glows

All of the other reindeer
Used to laugh and call him names
They never let poor Rudolf
Join in any reindeer games

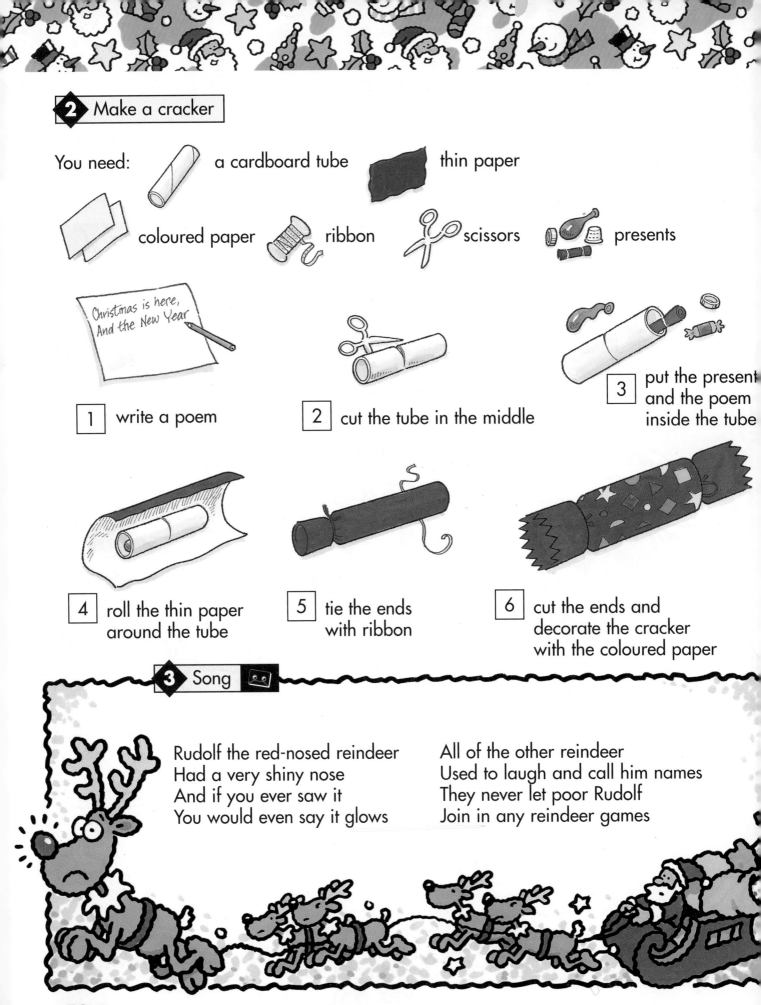

DO YOU KNOW THAT...?

 **1** Listen and read

1 In Great Britain, the 24th of December is Christmas Eve, the 25th is Christmas Day and the 26th is Boxing Day. On Christmas Day, families eat a big Christmas dinner.

2 The first Christmas cards date from 1840. British people send more than 1500 million cards every year.

3 The giant Christmas tree in Trafalgar Square, in the centre of London, is a present from the people of Norway to the people of Great Britain for their help during the Second World War.

4 Carols are the special songs people sing at Christmas time.

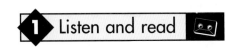

PANCAKE DAY

Pancake Day is on the Tuesday before Ash Wednesday. It is in February or at the beginning of March, six weeks before Easter.

In Britain, people eat pancakes on Pancake Day. In some towns there are pancake races. People run through the streets holding frying pans with pancakes. Each runner throws the pancake into the air and catches it in the pan.

In other countries, people celebrate Carnival at this time of the year. There are parades through the streets with bands, fireworks and people wearing masks and fancy dress.

2 Poem

1

2

3

4

5

6

Mix a pancake
Stir a pancake
Pop it in the pan

Fry the pancake
Toss the pancake
Catch it if you can!

3 Listen and glue in order   Cut out 6 Activity Book page 77

You need: scissors   glue   crayons

1   cut out

2   glue

The Big Pancake

3   colour

DO YOU KNOW THAT...?

 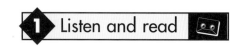

1 Another name for Pancake Day is Shrove Tuesday.

2 The world record for the biggest pancake is 15 metres in diameter, weighing 2980 kilos.

3 Carnival is an old Italian festival. In Venice at Carnival time there are great balls in the old palaces. People in fancy dress and masks go to the palaces in gondolas.

4 One of the most famous festivals is the Carnival of Rio de Janeiro in Brazil. Thousands of people go to Rio at Carnival.

THE SUPER BUS RACE

Add one more

1 Train, bicycle, boat, car …
2 Father, mother, brother, sister …
3 January, February, March, April …
4 Maths, Science, Geography, PE …
5 Two o'clock, a quarter past two, half past two, a quarter to three …
6 Thirsty, hungry, tired, happy …
7 Listen, write, speak, draw …

1 First, second, third, fourth …
2 Plastic bags, cans, tins, paper …
3 Richard, Steve, Paul, John …
4 The Moon, the Sun, comet, planet …
5 Half past one, a quarter to two, two o'clock, a quarter past two …
6 Stand up, come here, clean the blackboard, go out …
7 Football, basketball, tennis, swimming …

1 A, B, C, D …
2 Cold, hot, foggy, windy …
3 Julie, Karen, Sarah, Anna …
4 Headache, tummyache, earache, sore throat …
5 A quarter past one, half past one, a quarter to two, two o'clock …
6 Dog, rat, monster, spider …
7 Get up, have breakfast, go to school, have lunch …

FINISH

Macmillan Education
4 Crinan Street, London N1 9XW

A division of Macmillan Publishers Limited

Companies and representatives throughout the world

ISBN 13: 978 0 333 93167 7

Text © María José Lobo and Pepita Subirà 2000
Design and illustration © Macmillan Publishers Limited 2000
Heinemann is a trademark of Harcourt Education, used under licence.
First published 2000

Designed by COX DESIGN PARTNERSHIP, Witney, Oxon.

Cover illustration by Geo Parkin.

Illustrations by David Lock, Julie Anderson, Tony De Saulles, Karen Donnelly, John Haslam, Susan Hellard, Ann Johns, Derek Matthews, Kevin McAleenan, Geo Parkin.

Music by Tony Aitken.
Recordings produced by James Richardson.

Acknowledgements:
Dedicated to Mª José and Diego Carrión, Mireia and Núria Navas.

The authors would also like to thank Sue Bale, Karen Spiller, Rachael McMullen and Julie Stone, and all the people at Heinemann Iberia and Heinemann English Language Teaching. The authors would also like to thank Kate Melliss and James Styring for their involvement in the initial project.

The publishers would like to thank these children for drawing the posters and cards on pages 22 and 43: Nicola Heaver, Naomi Melliss and Eleanor Foreman-Peck.

The authors and publishers would like to thank Jaume Baldomà, C.P. Brasil, Barcelona; Remei Sánchez, C.P. Els Horts de al Verneda, Barcelona; Sossy De Swert, C.P. Nabí, Barcelona; Mª José Moyano, Escola Nausica, Barcelona; Gemma Carreras i Moratonas, Col.legi Orandai, Barcelona; Maite Fajardo, C.P. Arcipreste de Hita, Fuenlabrada; Montserrat Garcia, C.P. Arcipreste de Hita, Fuenlabrada; Pedro Romera, C.P. Manuel de Falla, Fuenlabrada; Manuel Fraile, C.P. Juan Pérez Villamil, Móstoles; Ros Mª Alaminos Arias, C.P. León Felipe, Móstoles; Angela Anta, C.P. Rafael Alberti, Móstoles; Carolina Molina, C.P. Rafael Alberti, Móstoles; Santiago Sánchez, C.P. Rafael Alberti, Móstoles; Julia de Miguel Camiruaga, C.P. El Casal, Abanto y Ciervana; José Mª Pizarro, C.P. Ingeniero José Orbegozo, Bilbao; Esmeralda Lopategui, C.P. Kareaga-Goikoa Asturi, Basauri; Azuzena Crespo, Colegio Sagrado Corazón, Bilbao; Begoña Latorre, C.P. Urreta, Galdacano; Eulalia Leza, C.P. Zabala Juan de Garay, Bilbao.

Commissioned photography by Chris Honeywell pp17, 18, 51(t)

Ajax/J Eastland pp31 (b,c), 32(5); Anthony Blake Photo Library pp51(bl), 56(b), 62(tl); Collections pp59(br), 60; S & R Greenhill p59(tl); Image Bank pp19(t), 38(br), 44(tr,bl), 62(bl); Impact p56(t); Rex Features p32(3); Science Photo Library pp18(t), 26(r); courtesy of Sony UK p18(b); Still Pictures pp44(br), 51(br); Stockfile p31(f); Tony Stone Images p18(b), 32(2,4); Telegraph Colour Library pp26(tl), 51(ml), 59(bl), 62(r); Trip & Art Directors pp31(e), 59(tr); Werner Forman Archive p12 (bl,br); John Walmsley p12(t); Melina Yakas p12(bc); Zefa Pictures pp26(ml,bl), 38(tl,tr,bl), 44(tl), 51(mr).

Poem "Mix a pancake" (page 58) written by Christina Rosetti. Reproduced by kind permission of A & C Black (Publishers) Limited.

"Rudolph the Red-nosed reindeer". Words & music by Johnny Marks © 1949, St Nicholas Music Inc., USA. Warner/Chappell Music Limited, London, W6 8BS. Reproduced by permission of IMP Limited.

Printed and bound in China.

2019   2018   2017   2016
20 19 18